THE BIG DIPPER and YOU

THE BIG DIPPER
and YOU

WRITTEN BY
E.C. KRUPP

ILLUSTRATED BY
ROBIN RECTOR KRUPP

North Star

MORROW JUNIOR BOOKS
NEW YORK

For Ethan,
Blake, Clark,
Carson,
and Kevin,
bright stars
we know and recognize

1 2 3 4 5 6 7 8 9 10

Library of Congress Cataloging-in-Publication Data
Krupp, E. C. (Edwin C.), 1944–
    The Big Dipper and you / by E.C. Krupp ; illus-
trated by Robin Rector Krupp.
      p.   cm.
    Summary: Presents what is known today and past
beliefs about the Big Dipper, or Ursa Major, and gives
added information on the North Star, or Polaris.
ISBN 0-688-07191-0. ISBN 0-688-07192-9 (lib. bdg.)
    1. Ursa Major—Juvenile literature.   2. Polestar
—Juvenile literature.   [1. Ursa Major. 2. Constellations. 3. Polestar. 4. Stars.]   I. Krupp, Robin
Rector, ill.   II. Title.
QB802.K78 1989
523.8—dc19   88-1501   CIP   AC

Almost everybody knows about the Big Dipper. It's a set of stars in the sky. To most people, those stars look like a dipper.

A dipper can be a helpful tool, but you don't see dippers around the house so much anymore. Your water is carried by pipes right to the sink. But if you lived in the country and had to get your water from a well, you would carry your water in a bucket and use a dipper to get a drink.

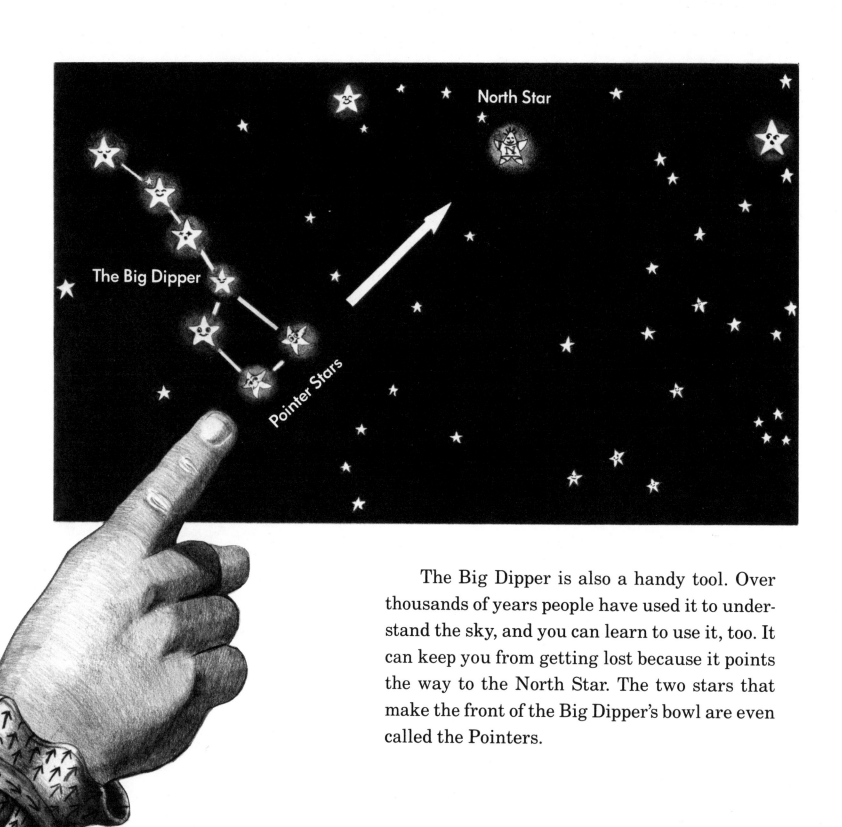

The Big Dipper is also a handy tool. Over thousands of years people have used it to understand the sky, and you can learn to use it, too. It can keep you from getting lost because it points the way to the North Star. The two stars that make the front of the Big Dipper's bowl are even called the Pointers.

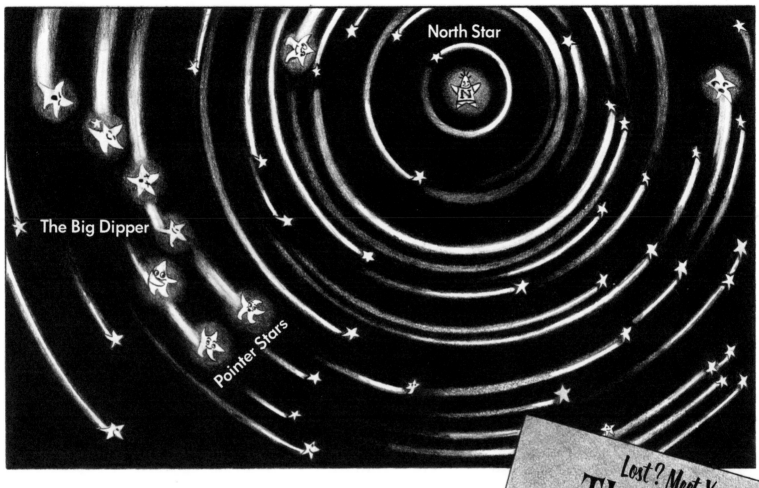

If you follow the invisible line that connects the two Pointers, you'll come to the North Star. The North Star is really special. Every other star follows its own trail through the sky, but the North Star stands still. It's the only star that does that. The whole sky seems to turn around it.

Lost? Meet Your Guide
The North Star

FREE!

RELIABLE!

HUNDREDS OF YEARS OF EXPERIENCE!

Easy Directions: Wait until dark. Follow the Pointers to the star that stands still.

Have you ever twirled an umbrella over your head? The sky looks like an umbrella with stars painted on the inside. If this umbrella had a handle, the top end of it would mark the North Star.

As the sky umbrella turns, new stars rise on one side of it. At the same time, different stars go down on the other side. But the stars that are close to the North Star do not rise or set. They just circle right around it. Where you live, most of the stars in the Big Dipper never set.

Stars set

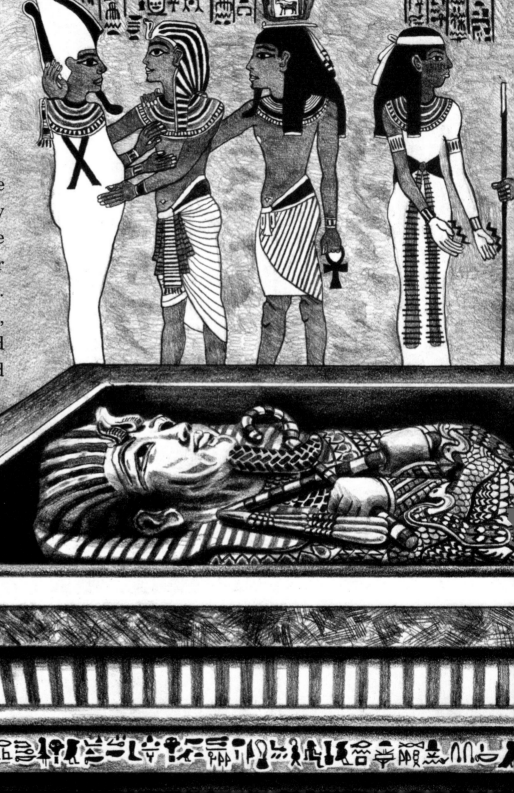

Because those stars never left the sky, the ancient Egyptians said they lived forever. They also believed the stars of the Big Dipper had the power to bring a mummy's spirit back to life. At funerals, an Egyptian priest, dressed in a leopard-skin robe, faced the mummy. The leopard's spots stood for the stars of the night sky.

The priest carried a hook in his hand. It was shaped like the Big Dipper, and it stood for the stars that never died. When the priest touched the mummy's mouth with this magical hook, the Egyptians believed it gave the mummy's spirit the breath of life.

King Tutankhamun's tomb

North Star

If you could see the Big Dipper in the daytime, you would see it go completely around the North Star in 24 hours. Of course, it's not really the Big Dipper that is moving. It's the earth. The earth is shaped like a ball, and it spins like a merry-go-round.

On a merry-go-round pony, you move about 10 miles per hour. On the turning earth, you travel 800 miles per hour. Even though the earth turns a lot faster, you don't feel it. That's because the earth doesn't start and stop as a merry-go-round does. Because you don't feel the earth turn, it looks as if the sky moves.

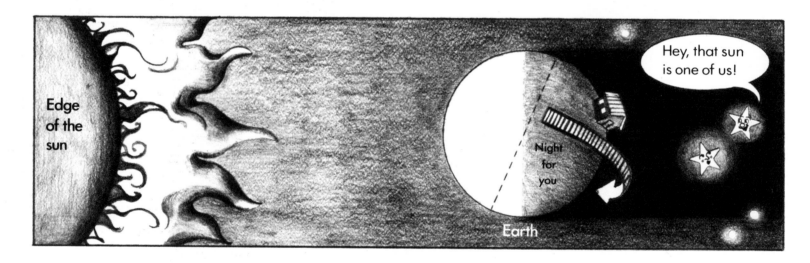

In 24 hours the earth spins around once. That's why we have day and night. The sun is always there in outer space, but you see it only when your side of the earth faces it. At night you see stars. The sun is a star, too, but it is much closer to us than all of the other stars. That is why it looks so much bigger and brighter.

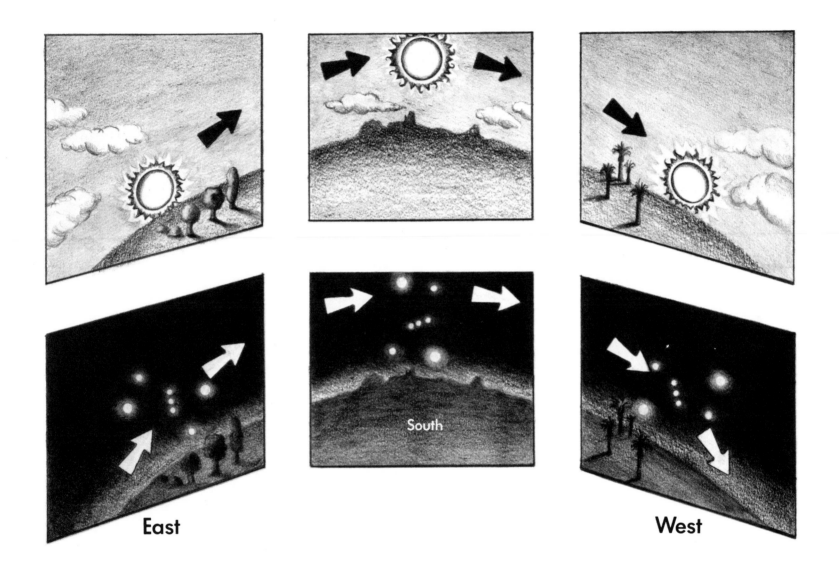

East

South

West

When you first see the sun in the morning, your spot on the earth has just started to face the sun. As the day goes by, the spinning earth turns you past the sun. It's highest at noon. Your last view of the sun comes at sunset. The earth is turning you away from the sun. At night, stars rise and set the same way the sun does in the daytime because the earth is turning past them, too.

Balls spin, and so do the wheels on cars and toys. Each wheel has an axle that goes through its center. The spinning earth has something like an axle, too, but it is just an imaginary line. It is called the earth's axis, and it goes through the earth's center. The North Pole is at one end of the axis, and the South Pole is at the other. A hubcap covers the end of the axle on the wheel of a car. If you were going to cover both ends of the earth's axis, you would put a hubcap on top of each pole.

North Pole

Axis of the earth

South Pole

16

Have you ever been to the North Pole? Probably not. It's pretty far and very cold. Of course, there is no hubcap on top of the North Pole. And there is no real pole there. But if there were, it would point straight up and toward the North Star. That is why the North Star is sometimes called the Pole Star. It's also called Polaris, and that means the same thing—Pole Star.

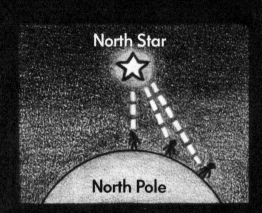

North Star

North Pole

Back where you live, you don't see the North Star straight above you at night. That's because the earth is round. As you travel farther from the earth's North Pole, the North Star slips lower in the sky. It's not so easy to spot it. It's not the brightest star in your sky. There are 49 brighter ones. That's why you need the Big Dipper. It's your compass. A compass needle points north, and the Big Dipper points to the North Star.

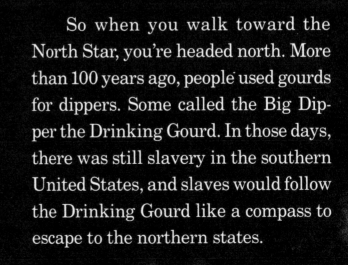

So when you walk toward the North Star, you're headed north. More than 100 years ago, people used gourds for dippers. Some called the Big Dipper the Drinking Gourd. In those days, there was still slavery in the southern United States, and slaves would follow the Drinking Gourd like a compass to escape to the northern states.

19

Even though the height of the North Star may be different, it's always in the same direction: north. And once you know where north is, you will know the other directions, too. South is just the opposite direction. And east and west are halfway between north and south.

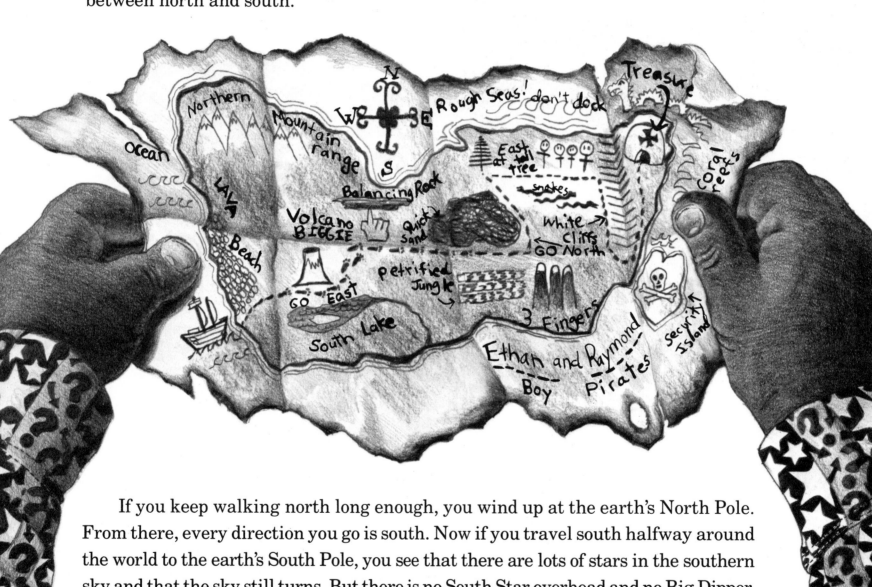

If you keep walking north long enough, you wind up at the earth's North Pole. From there, every direction you go is south. Now if you travel south halfway around the world to the earth's South Pole, you see that there are lots of stars in the southern sky and that the sky still turns. But there is no South Star overhead and no Big Dipper, either.

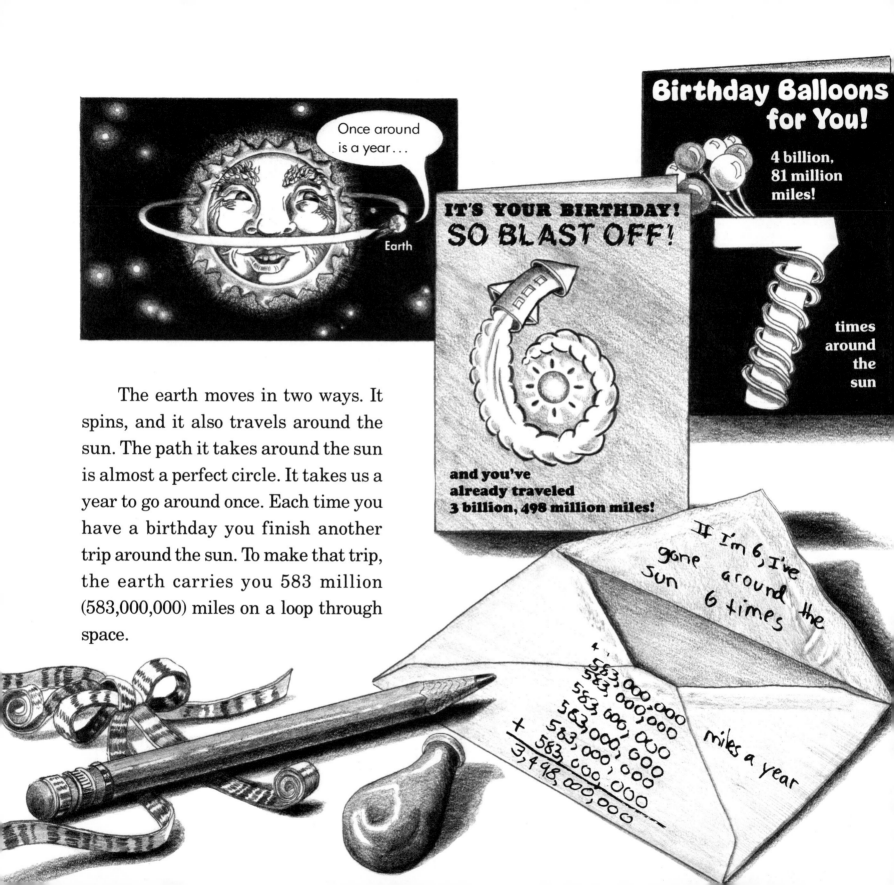

The earth moves in two ways. It spins, and it also travels around the sun. The path it takes around the sun is almost a perfect circle. It takes us a year to go around once. Each time you have a birthday you finish another trip around the sun. To make that trip, the earth carries you 583 million (583,000,000) miles on a loop through space.

23

To go that far in a single year, you have to move pretty fast. The earth does move fast. It circles the sun at about 67,000 miles per hour. No airplane can reach that speed. Not even the Apollo spacecraft that went to the moon could do that. Its top speed was 25,000 miles per hour.

Start counting days the first day after your birthday...

Keep going

SPEED LIMIT EARTH

67,000 MILES PER HOUR

SPEED LIMIT APOLLO

25,000 MILES PER HOUR

You can't feel the earth moving, though. It spins around 365 times—once each day—and travels completely around the sun every year, and you don't feel a thing. But you can feel the seasons change. In summer it is hot, and in winter it is cold.

ur next birthday... That's a year, or 365 days...

Earth

But you aren't really closer to the sun in summer. And you're not really farther from the sun in winter. The earth's path is almost a perfect circle. That means you are almost always the same distance from the sun.

25

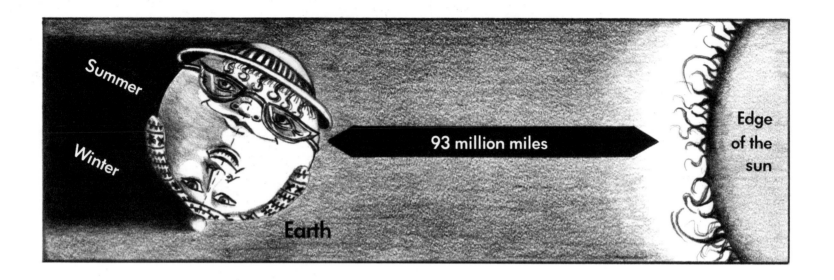

Summer

Winter

93 million miles

Earth

Edge of the sun

So why do we have seasons? The earth is tilted over, that's why. It stays tilted in the same direction during the entire trip around the sun. So all through the year you see the North Star in the same place. But during part of the year, your half of the earth is tipped toward the sun. The sun shines straight on it and heats it up more quickly. It is summer then, and your ice cream melts. The sun's path is high. It doesn't get dark until late, and you have to wait to see the Big Dipper.

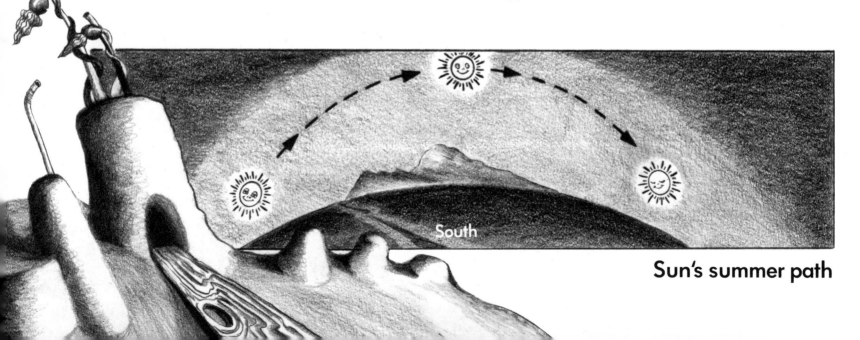

South

Sun's summer path

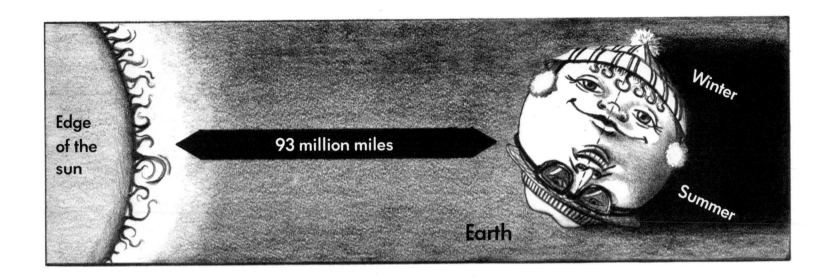

Edge of the sun

93 million miles

Winter

Summer

Earth

In winter, the other half of the earth is tilted toward the sun. Now it is summer there, but it is winter where you live. The sun's light comes in at a low slant. It can't heat the earth where you are as well as it did before. It's colder than it was six months ago. Also, you can't play outside so late because the sun's low path across the sky makes the days shorter. Now it gets dark early, and you can see the Big Dipper sooner.

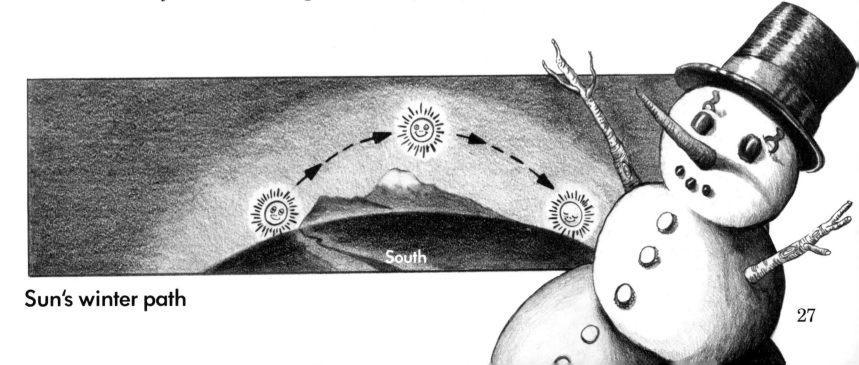

South

Sun's winter path

Sometime

Sometime later that night

Now we know our earth has two motions in space. It spins like a merry-go-round, and it journeys around the sun. Each of these two motions makes the Big Dipper seem to move in the sky. One motion turns the Big Dipper into a clock, and the other turns it into a calendar.

The spinning earth makes the Big Dipper move around the North Star like a hand on a clock—but in the other direction. The handle shows how the hours pass, and you can use it to tell time at night.

The Big Dipper circles the North Star once every 24 hours.

Because the earth travels around the sun, the seasons change, and so does the Big Dipper. That's why you can use it like a calendar. The Yi People, in southwest China, notice which way the Big Dipper faces at the same time each night. That changes during the year. They start their calendar in winter, when the bowl of the Dipper is high and opens toward the side.

HAPPY NEW YEAR

29

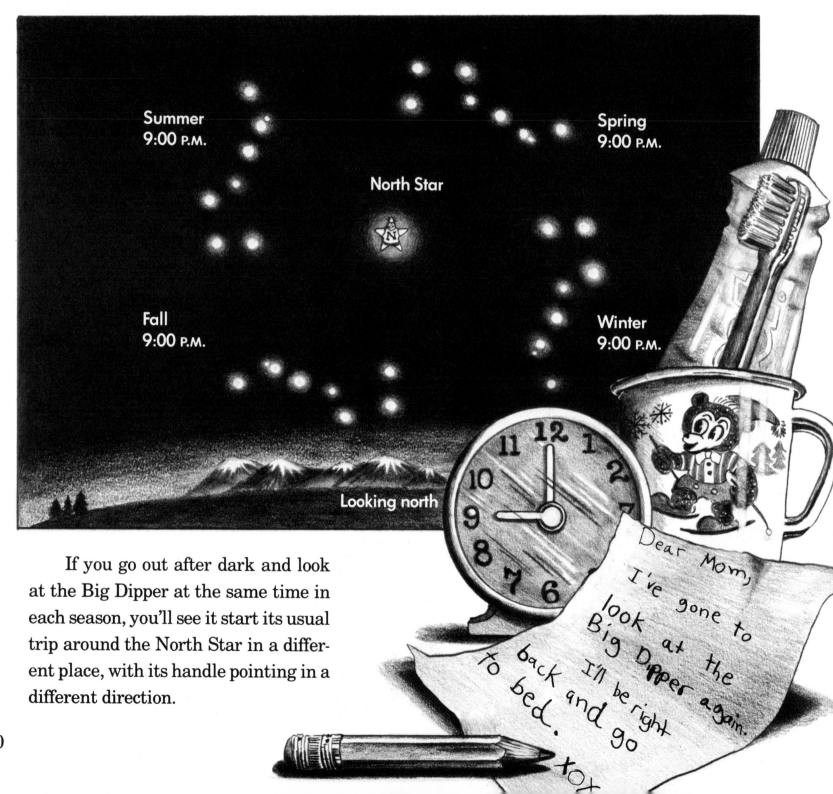

Summer
9:00 P.M.

Spring
9:00 P.M.

North Star

Fall
9:00 P.M.

Winter
9:00 P.M.

Looking north

Dear Mom,
I've gone to look at the Big Dipper again. I'll be right back and go to bed.
xox

If you go out after dark and look at the Big Dipper at the same time in each season, you'll see it start its usual trip around the North Star in a different place, with its handle pointing in a different direction.

In spring, you'll see the Big Dipper up above the North Star. The bowl faces the ground. If there were water in the Big Dipper, it would pour straight down like rain and water the spring flowers.

In summer, look for the Big Dipper to the left of the North Star. The handle is high, and the bowl is low. On hot summer nights, it would be handy to have a dipper full of cold lemonade.

In fall, the bowl of the Big Dipper slides along the ground. If you could fill it with water now, you could bob for apples in it.

In winter, the Big Dipper's handle hangs down like an icicle. Now you find the Dipper to the right of the North Star. Make sure you dress warmly if you go look for it.

Canadian jay

Blue jay

Great horned owl

Saw-whet owl

The Micmac Indians in Canada knew that the Big Dipper started the night in a new spot each season. For them, the Dipper's bowl was a bear. It prowled around the North Star. The bear was chased by the three bright stars in the Dipper's handle and by four other stars nearby. They are in a group we sometimes call the Herdsman. These hunters, the Indians said, were really birds. When they caught the bear in the fall, they shot it with an arrow, and its blood turned the leaves of the trees red.

Pigeon

Chickadee

Robin

People have been watching the Big Dipper for thousands of years. The Vikings called it a wagon because it traveled around the sky.

In China, it was a chariot that carried the king of the sky.

They still call it a plough in England.

The Hindus of India say the Dipper's seven bright stars are seven wise men.

You can see another dipper near the Big Dipper. It's called the Little Dipper, and the North Star is at the end of its handle. The ancient Greeks called this group of stars the Small Bear. Does it look like a bear to you? Not much. Bears don't have long tails. They called it the Small Bear, though, because they saw a bigger bear in the sky. That bear included the stars we call the Big Dipper, and their name for it was the Great Bear. Groups of stars like the Great Bear and the Small Bear are known as constellations. Astronomers are scientists who study the stars, and they still use an ancient name for the constellation that includes the Big Dipper. They call it Ursa Major. That just means Great Bear. Their name for the Little Dipper is Ursa Minor, or Small Bear.

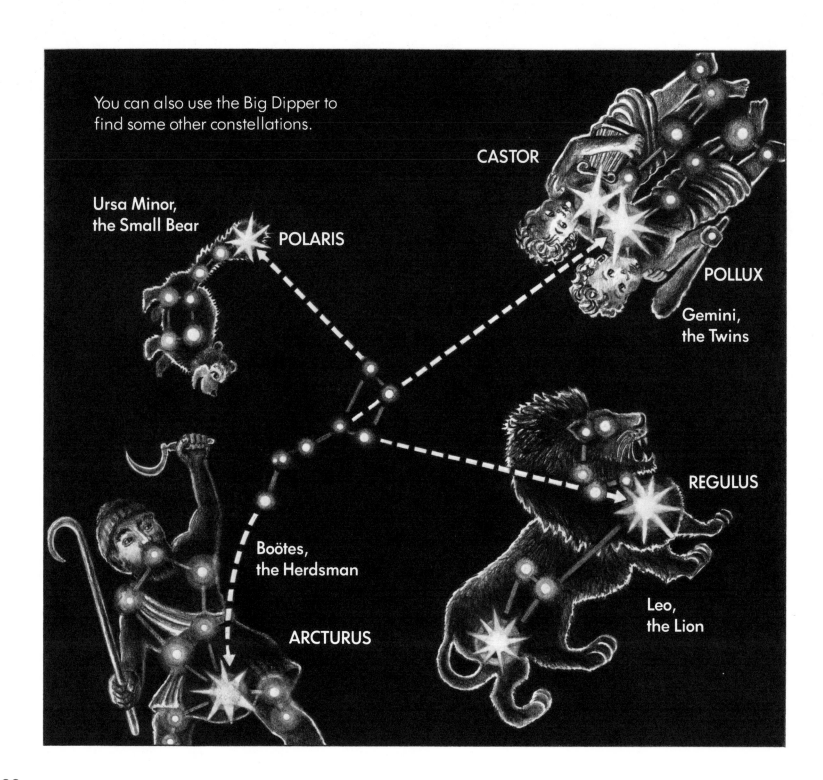

You can also use the Big Dipper to find some other constellations.

CASTOR

Ursa Minor, the Small Bear

POLARIS

POLLUX

Gemini, the Twins

Boötes, the Herdsman

REGULUS

Leo, the Lion

ARCTURUS

When you look up at the sky, you can't tell how far away the stars really are. The stars in the Big Dipper look like they are all together in one place, and two of them look like they are really close together. To spot them, look carefully at the second star from the end of the Big Dipper's handle. You'll see another star right next to it. It is much fainter, and it may be hard to find it. Hundreds of years ago, the Arabs and the Persians used that star to test how sharply their eyes could see. Can you pick it out tonight?

That faint star is named Alcor, and the bright one near it is called Mizar. They look like they are close together, but Alcor is much farther away. None of the stars of the Big Dipper is really close to the others.

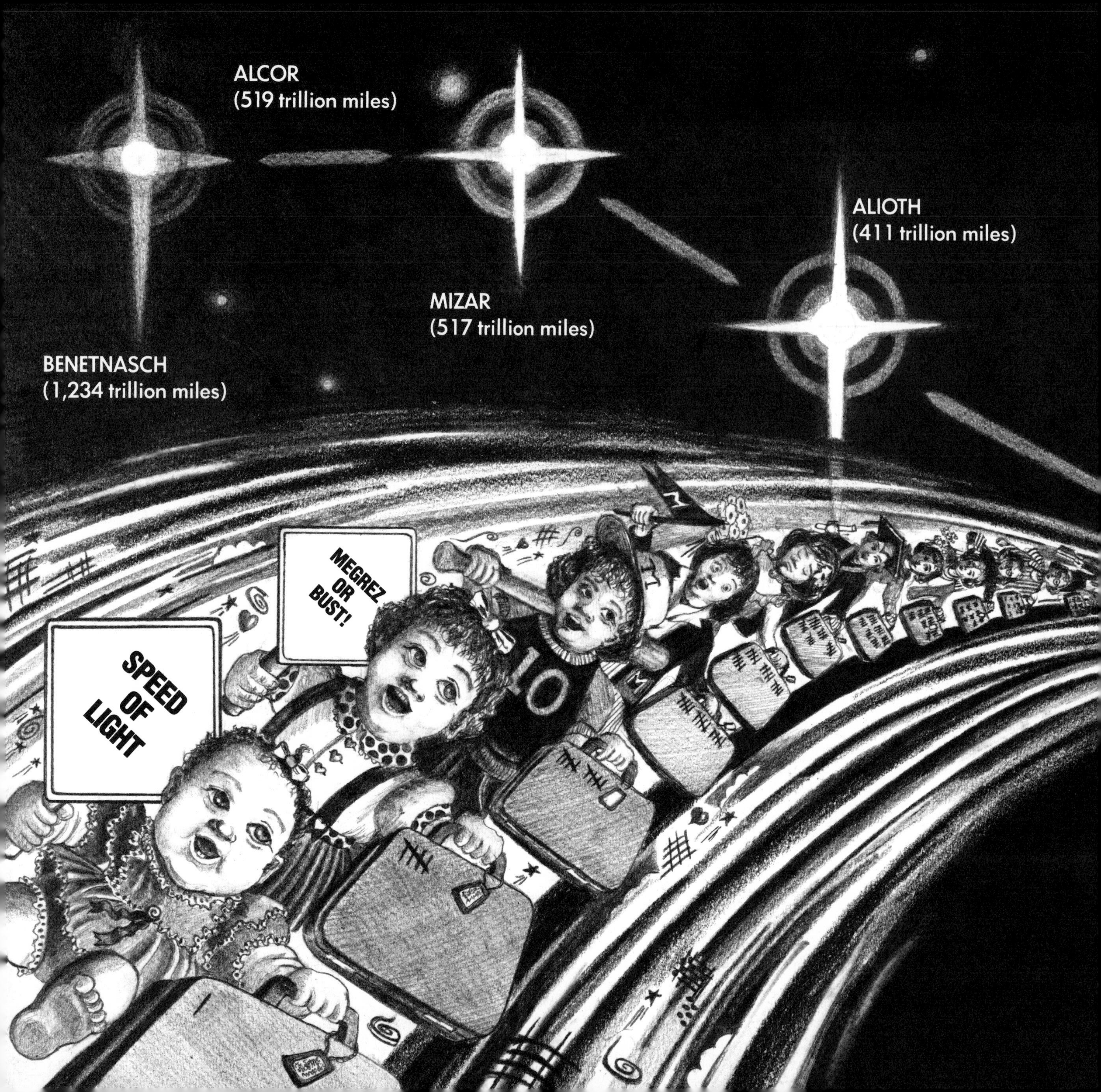
ALCOR
(519 trillion miles)
ALIOTH
(411 trillion miles)
MIZAR
(517 trillion miles)
BENETNASCH
(1,234 trillion miles)
MEGREZ OR BUST!
SPEED OF LIGHT
10

If you took off in a spaceship toward the stars of the Big Dipper, you would first reach the one that marks the corner of the bowl that connects with the Dipper's handle. Its name is Megrez.

Our fastest space probes, *Voyagers 1* and *2*, have traveled to the outer planets that circle around our sun, but they are nowhere near as far away as even the closest star. If your spaceship could go as fast as the *Voyagers*, it would still take you 10 billion (10,000,000,000) years to get to Megrez. That's twice as long as the age of our own earth. Even if you could travel at the speed of light, the fastest anything can go, it would take 65 years to get to that star. If you left when you were born, you would arrive in time to retire.

Once you arrive at Megrez, you'll find that the seven stars in the Big Dipper don't look like a dipper anymore. Even from the earth they won't always look like a dipper. And they haven't always looked like the same dipper in the past.

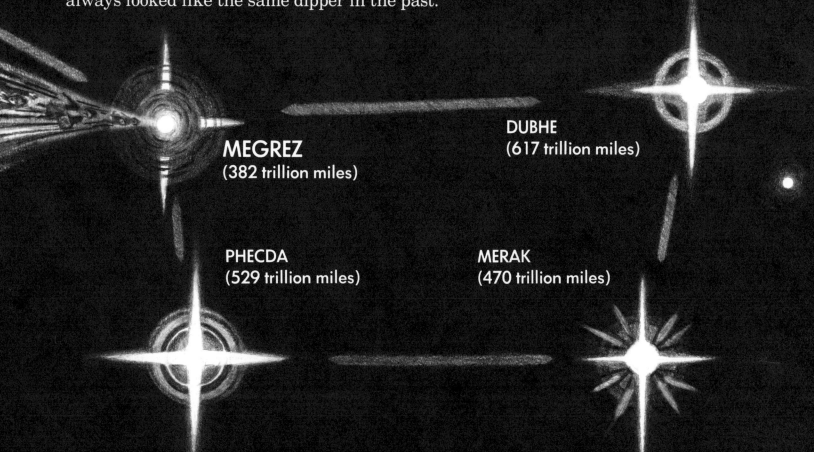

MEGREZ
(382 trillion miles)

DUBHE
(617 trillion miles)

PHECDA
(529 trillion miles)

MERAK
(470 trillion miles)

100,000 years ago

Now

100,000 years from now

When early Neanderthal people looked at the Big Dipper 100,000 years ago, they saw it with a straight handle and a small bowl. That's because five of the stars are moving through space in one direction, and the other two are headed elsewhere. If they were all going in the same direction, the Dipper wouldn't change much at all. Instead, they are going away from each other at a speed of tens of thousands of miles per hour. That sounds fast, but because they are all so far away from us, it still takes a long time to see the change. But if you wait 100,000 years, the handle will be bent down, and the front of the bowl will be flopped open.

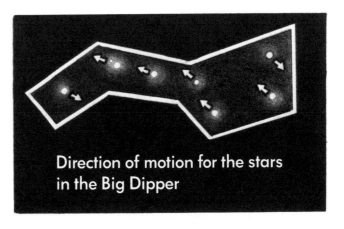

Direction of motion for the stars in the Big Dipper

So our Big Dipper won't always look like a dipper. And for a different reason, Polaris won't always be a North Star. It hasn't always been the North Star, either. Back at the time the Egyptians were building the pyramids, their North Star was Thuban, in the constellation Draco the Dragon. After that, there wasn't a North Star for a long time. And we'll have to wait a long time to get a new North Star after we lose the one we have now.

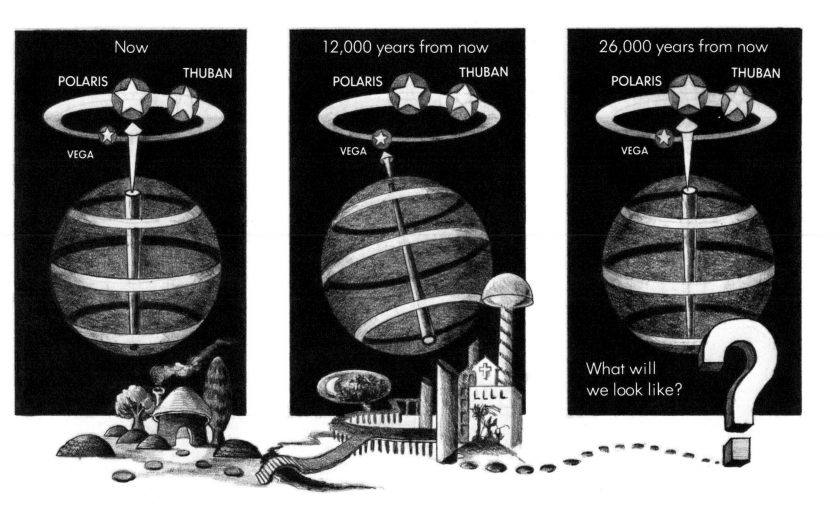

Thousands of years from now the bright star Vega, in Lyra the Harp, will become the new North Star. Vega, Polaris, and Thuban take turns at being the North Star every 26,000 years. The last time Polaris was the North Star, Ice Age hunters were tracking bison and mammoths. Although Polaris is the North Star now, it will slowly drift away from its familiar place in the sky. It will gradually circle back in 26,000 years, however, when it will have the North Star job again. Each night the sky still seems to turn around one special spot, but over thousands of years that spot moves from one North Star to another. Why does the North Star change?

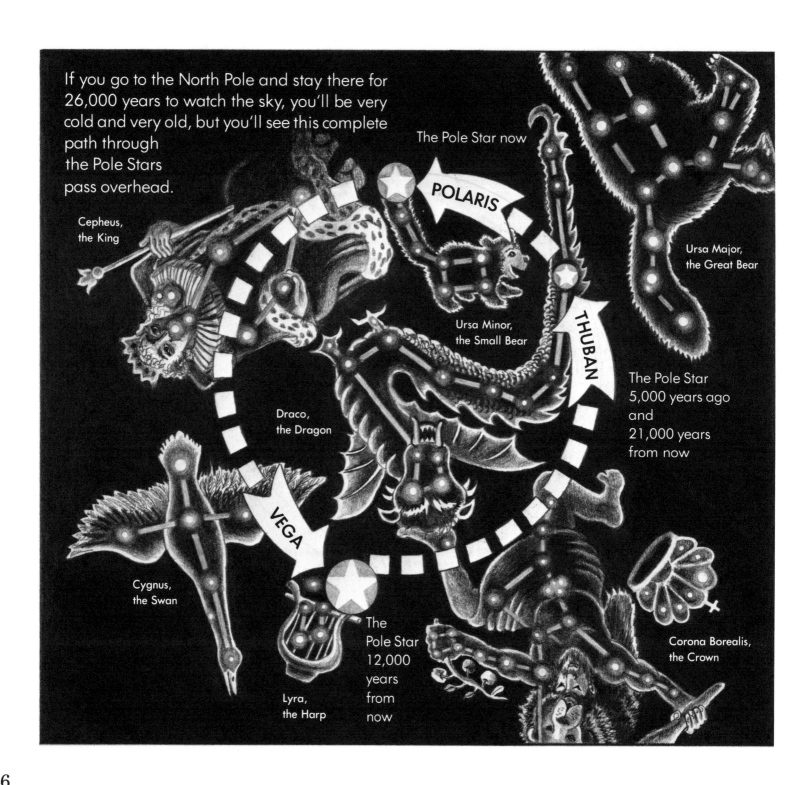

If you go to the North Pole and stay there for 26,000 years to watch the sky, you'll be very cold and very old, but you'll see this complete path through the Pole Stars pass overhead.

The Pole Star now

POLARIS

Cepheus, the King

Ursa Major, the Great Bear

THUBAN

Ursa Minor, the Small Bear

The Pole Star 5,000 years ago and 21,000 years from now

Draco, the Dragon

VEGA

Cygnus, the Swan

The Pole Star 12,000 years from now

Corona Borealis, the Crown

Lyra, the Harp

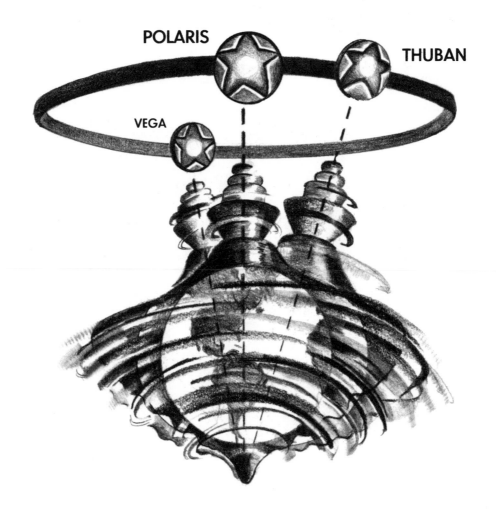

POLARIS

THUBAN

VEGA

It's not the North Star's own travel through space that makes this happen. It does move through space, but it is more than five times farther from us than Megrez. The North Star's great distance makes it look as if it's hardly traveling at all. So something else must be making it drift away.

The wobbling earth is what will give us a new North Star. As the earth spins, it also wobbles. So does a top. It swivels around while it turns. It takes a top only a second or so to wobble around once. But the earth's wobble is much slower. It tips the earth's North Pole around a circle through the stars, and it takes 26,000 years to close the loop once.

The earth is still tilted toward Polaris now. Tonight, Polaris is your North Star, and the Big Dipper helps you find it. The way the Big Dipper turns through the night and the way it follows the seasons through the year help you understand the sky. Tonight, the Big Dipper is your calendar, compass, and clock. It makes you feel at home.